# STORYVILLE PRESENTS

# DUKE ELLINGTON

## THE ORIGINAL PIANO TRANSCRIPTIONS

**WISE PUBLICATIONS**
part of The Music Sales Group

London / New York / Paris / Sydney / Copenhagen / Berlin / Madrid / Hong Kong / Tokyo

Published by
Wise Publications
14/15 Berners Street, London W1T 3LJ, UK.

Exclusive distributors:
Music Sales Limited
Distribution Centre, Newmarket Road,
Bury St Edmunds, Suffolk IP33 3YB, UK.

Music Sales Pty Limited
20 Resolution Drive, Caringbah, NSW 2229, Australia.

Order No. AM1000021
ISBN 978-1-84938-474-2

This book © Copyright 2010 Wise Publications,
a division of Music Sales Limited.

Arranged and engraved by Camden Music.
Project editor: Ann Barkway.
Cover photograph & page 6 LFI.
Photographs page 3 Giles Petard/Redferns,
page 4, 5, 7 Michael Ochs Archive/Getty Images.

Printed in the EU.

www.musicsales.com

Your Guarantee of Quality:
As publishers, we strive to produce every book
to the highest commercial standards.

The music has been freshly engraved and the book has been
carefully designed to minimise awkward page turns and to make
playing from it a real pleasure. Particular care has been given
to specifying acid-free, neutral-sized paper made from pulps
which have not been elemental chlorine bleached.

This pulp is from farmed sustainable forests and
was produced with special regard for the environment.

Throughout, the printing and binding have been planned
to ensure a sturdy, attractive publication which should give
years of enjoyment.

If your copy fails to meet our high standards, please inform us
and we will gladly replace it.

# DUKE ELLINGTON

Born: 29 April 1899, Washington, DC, USA
Died: 24 May 1974, New York, NY, USA

Born to a middle-class family in Washington, DC, Edward Kennedy Ellington ('Duke' was a childhood nickname that reflected – or reinforced – his naturally rather patrician personality) began studying the piano at the age of seven. At first more interested in baseball than piano and demonstrating a flair for art during his high school years, Ellington soon gravitated back to music, mainly inspired by the ragtime players he heard in a local poolroom. At the age of 15, while working as a soda jerk in a café, he wrote his first ever piece, 'Soda Fountain Rag'. With help from a Washington pianist and band leader called Oliver 'Doc' Perry, he learned to read music and refine his technique.

Eventually he turned down an art scholarship to the Pratt Institute in Brooklyn in 1916 and began to perform music professionally, at first for other bands and then heading his own troupe, Duke's Syncopators. They built up a respectable performing circuit in and around Washington DC before venturing to play further afield. Eventually Duke Ellington and some musician friends went to New York where their attempts to graduate from playing cheap Harlem rent parties to cracking the professional jazz circuit at first met with failure. They went back to Washington to regroup.

A second attempt proved more successful resulting in stints with Elmer Snowden and his Black Sox Orchestra at The Exclusive Club in Harlem, then a four-year engagement at The Hollywood Club. Snowden left the group in early 1924 and Ellington took over as bandleader. When The Hollywood Club suffered a fire and was subsequently relaunched as Club Kentucky, Duke Ellington found the professional springboard he needed. In 1927 he landed the 'house band' engagement at Harlem's Cotton Club, playing for all of the revues and burlesque it staged.

Between 1932 and 1942 Ellington's career and musical inventiveness thrived as his band grew, accommodating some great jazz players. After a hiatus and a return home occasioned by the death of his mother, Ellington returned to New York and soon won another engagement at Cotton Club (now relocated in Manhattan's midtown). Throughout the previous decade his band had enjoyed some solid hits, none more famous than 'Take The 'A' Train', a composition by pianist Billy Strayhorn which became the band's signature tune and is included in this collection. The usual story about the famous title is that the 'A' train links Harlem, where all the black musicians used to live, with downtown Manhattan, where all the jazz clubs were. The 'A' train therefore became the informal commuter train for jazz musicians, taking them to the area where the work was to be found.

Another version of the story suggested that the title came from Ellington's directions to Strayhorn about how to get to his Harlem apartment; yet another has it that the title was a reminder to Harlem's Sugar Hill housewives to return home on the 'A' train as opposed to the 'D' train which swerves off to the east and The Bronx at 145th Street instead of continuing north to Harlem's Sugar Hill neighbourhood.

Whatever the true story it brought fame to Strayhorn, a man whom Ellington unfailingly praised and credited with closely sharing his own musical instincts and vision; the authorship of 'Satin Doll' (also featured on this collection) goes to Ellington although some believe Strayhorn wrote the melody. In 1937 the band's trombonist Juan Tizol wrote 'Caravan' which was also a hit for the Ellington band and stands as the first Latin or Middle East-influenced jazz song.

Ellington's residencies at the Cotton Club in Harlem had also prompted him to enlarge and expand his personnel and his compositional ambitions. With the help of first-rate musicians he broke away from the conventions of band-section scoring and instead deployed new harmonies to blend their individual sounds and create subtle moods with ingenious and unlikely combinations of instruments. Sometimes he composed pieces expressly to showcase his musicians in innovative groupings. Ellington's endless quest for musical advance would inform the remainder of his long career. Fascinating glimpses of that career are to be seen in this collection.

The earliest track featured comes from transcripts of three radio broadcasts made during a six-month engagement at the Hurricane Club in New York City in 1943 – Ellington's first New York residency since he first played the Cotton Club in 1938. 'Don't Get Around Much Anymore', a 1940 Ellington composition with lyrics by Bob Russell that were added only the year before this recording, was to become a jazz and popular music standard.

'Caravan', 'C' Jam Blues' and 'Cotton Tail' are all recordings of live performances made in 1949 at The Hollywood Empire in Los Angeles that were preserved on transcription discs for radio use. The 1949 line-up includes Ellington luminaries Billy Strayhorn, Ben Webster, Johnny Hodges and Ray Nance.

All other featured numbers date from the 1960s and were recorded in France or New York during a period when Ellington, now well-rewarded by royalties from his past work, was bringing ever more focus to composition, recording and performance. Still giving primacy to the sympathetic melding of music and performer, he disdained trends and arbitrary musical influences. As he observed in these later years, 'I think too strongly in terms of altering my music to fit the performer to be impressed by accidental music. You can't take doodling seriously'.

Ellington was one of nature's aristocrats who faced as much racial prejudice as any other black performer born in the American south at the start of the 20th century, but he dealt with it with quiet dignity and by producing a body of unarguably superb jazz...or 'American music' as he preferred to call it. He even left some characteristically urbane last words: 'Music is how I live, why I live and how I will be remembered.

# Blues #1

Music by Duke Ellington
Arranged by Jeremy Birchall

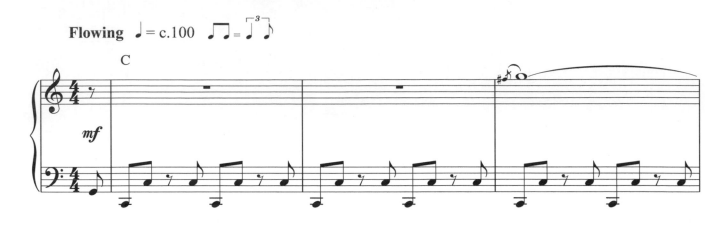

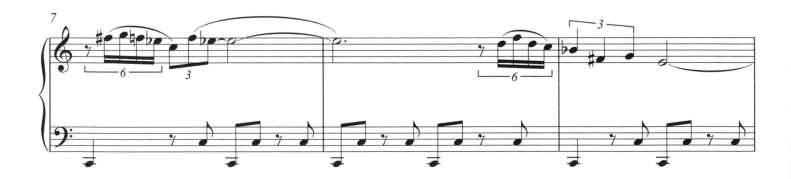

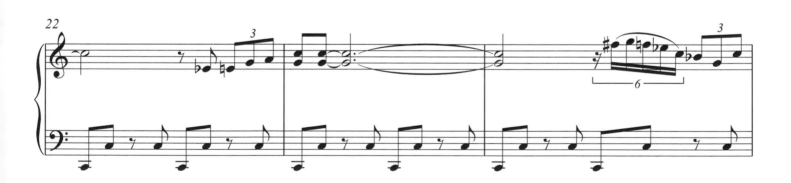

**molto rubato sempre**

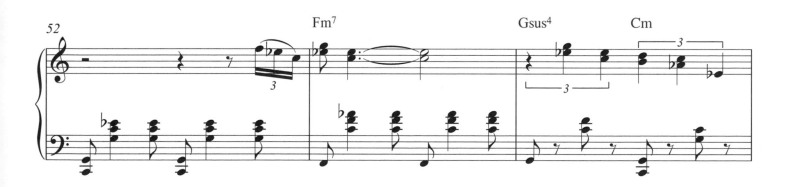

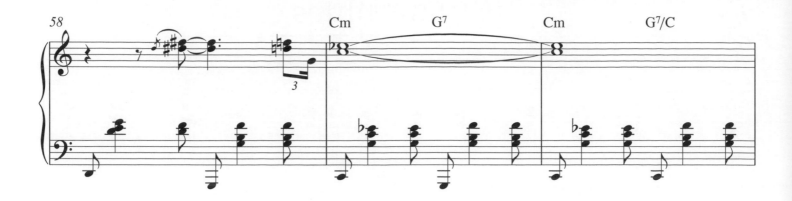

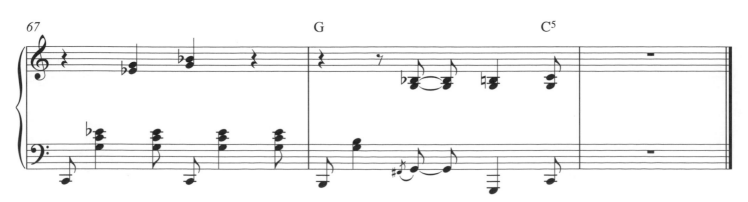

# 'C' Jam Blues

Music by Duke Ellington

Arranged by Jeremy Birchall

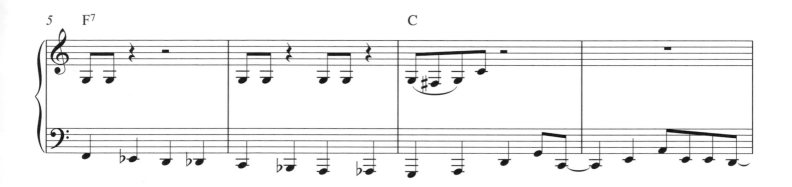

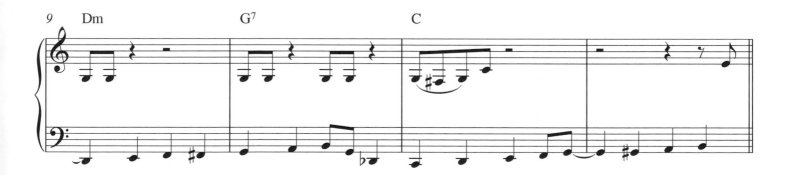

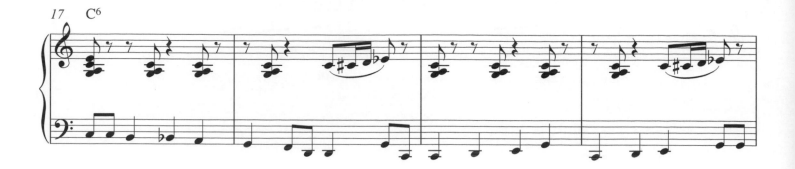

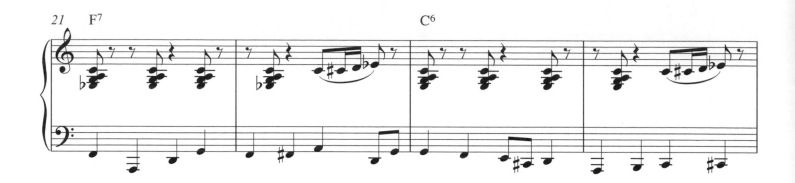

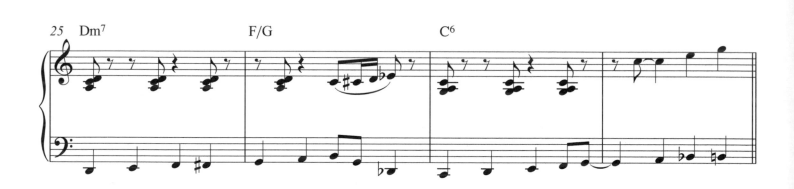

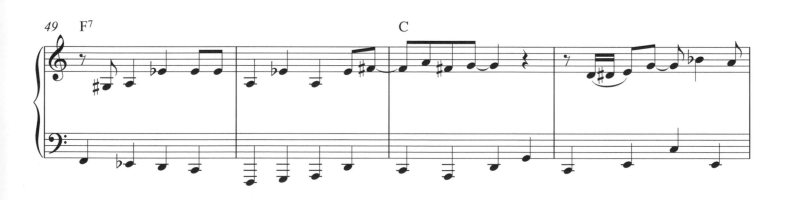

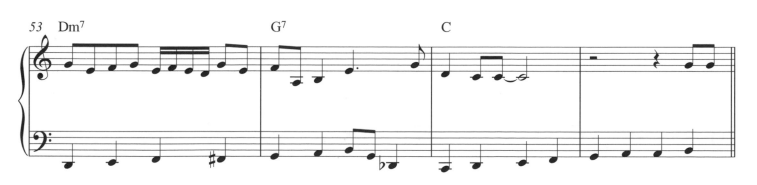

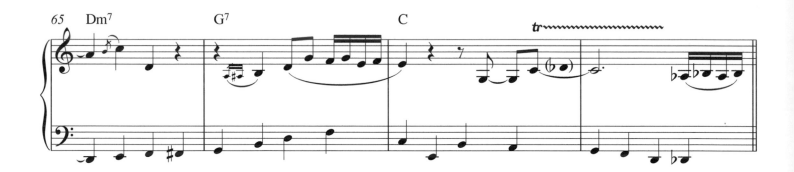

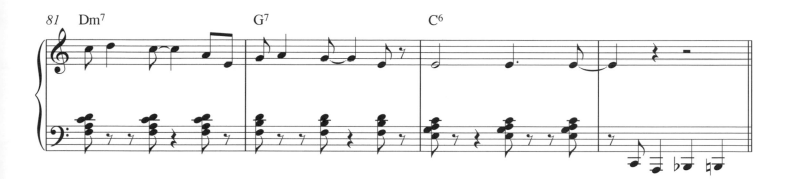

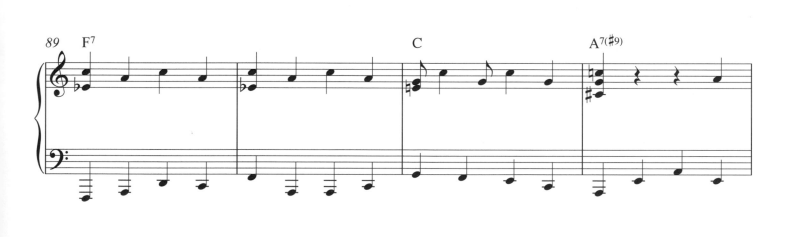

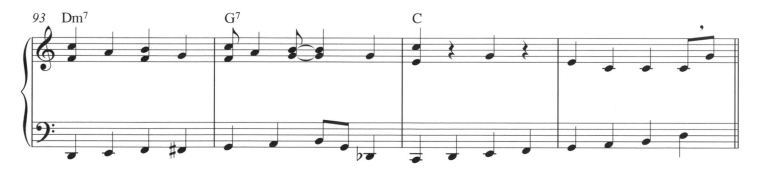

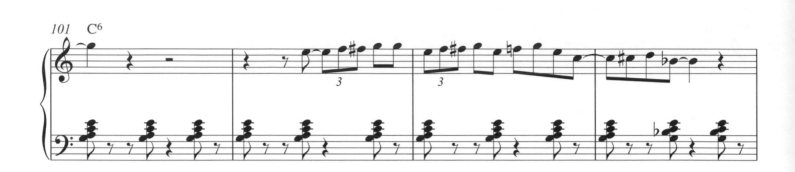

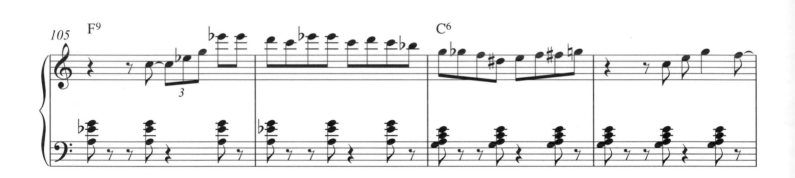

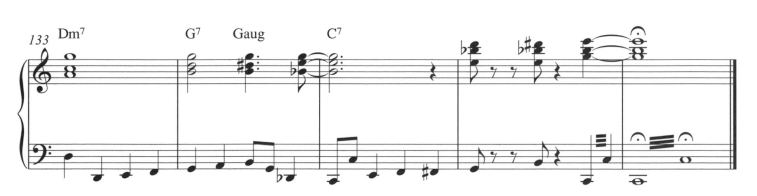

# Caravan

Words by Irving Mills & Music by Duke Ellington & Juan Tizol

Arranged by Carl Hudson

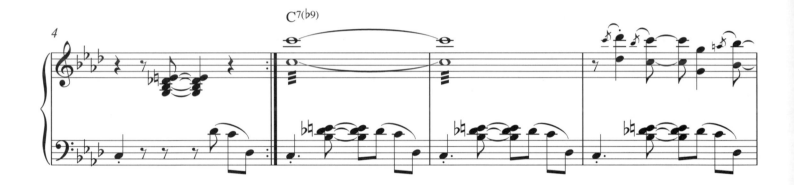

**Latin, with a lilt**  [straight 8s]

**to Coda** ⊕

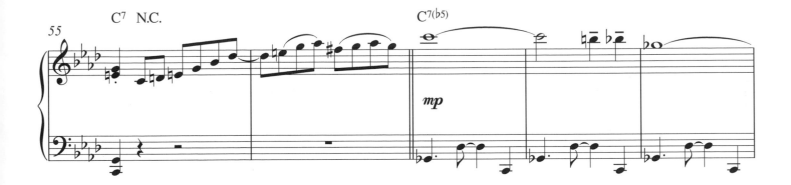

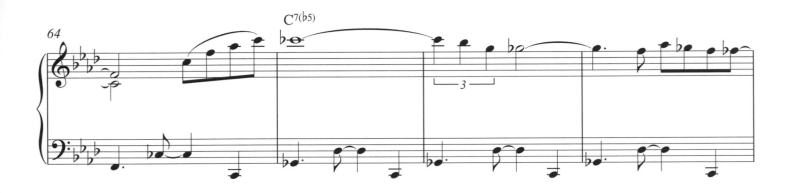

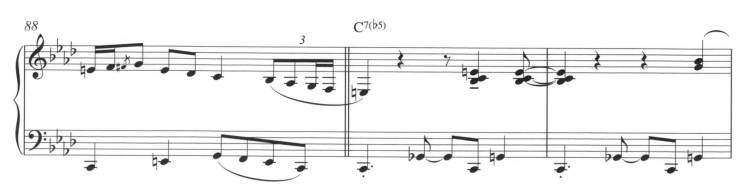

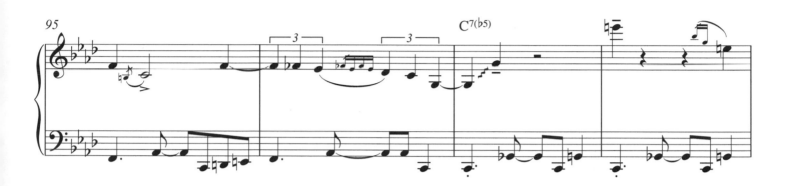

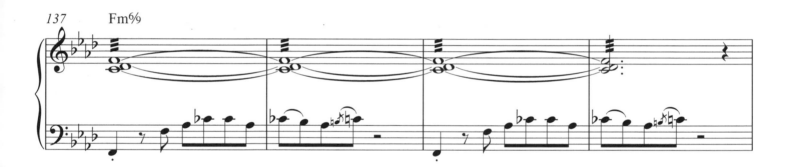

(black note gliss.)

# Cotton Tail

Music by Duke Ellington
Arranged by Jeremy Birchall

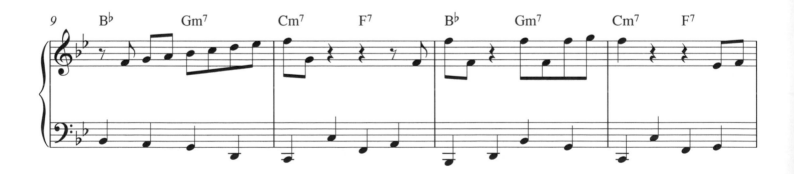

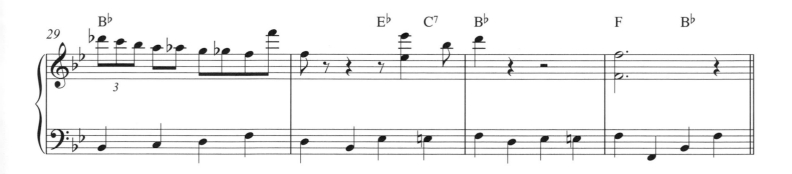

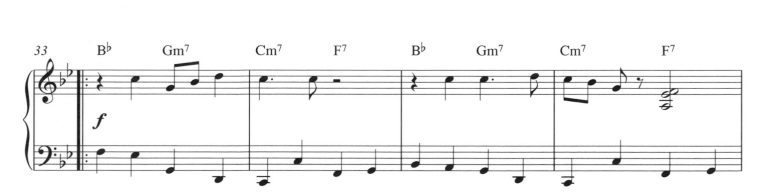

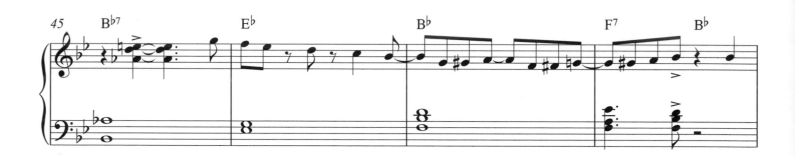

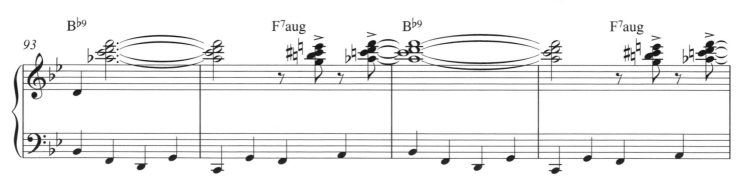

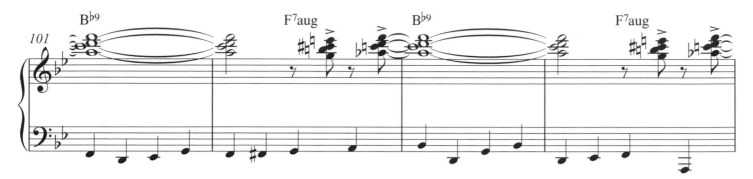

# Don't Get Around Much Anymore

Words by Bob Russell & Music by Duke Ellington
Arranged by Mark Lloyd

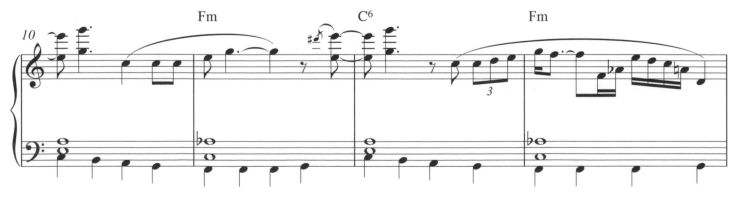

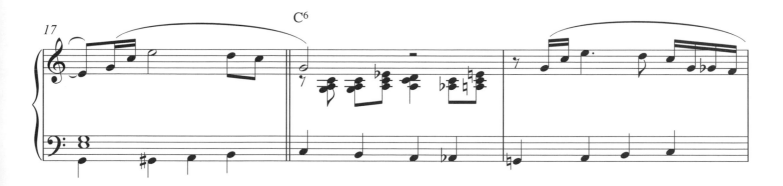

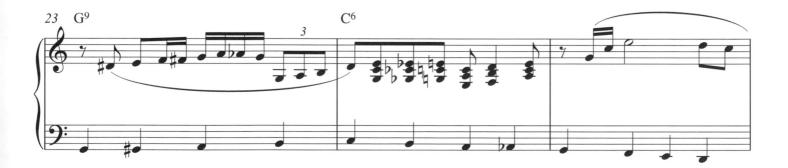

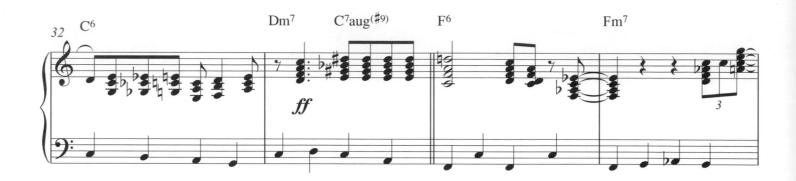

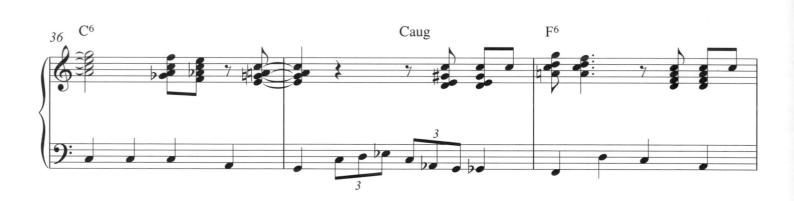

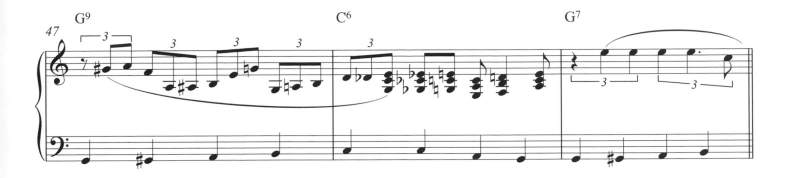

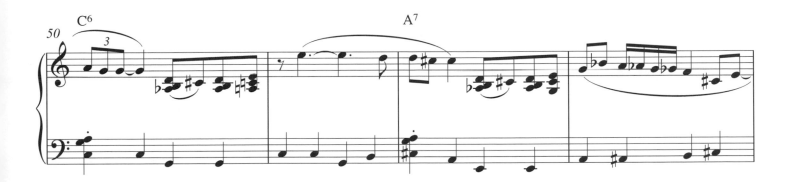

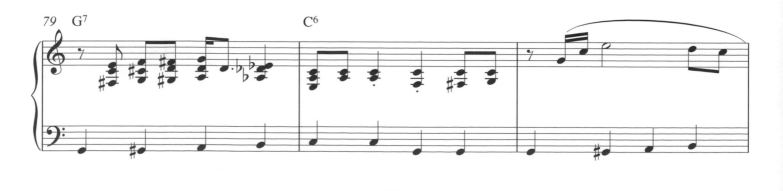

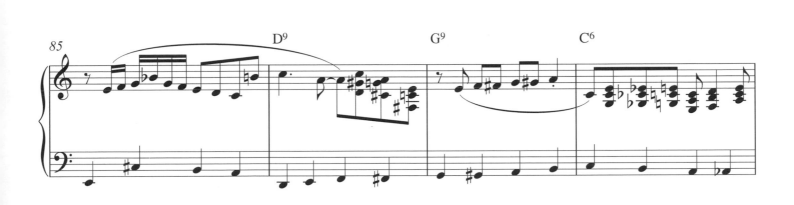

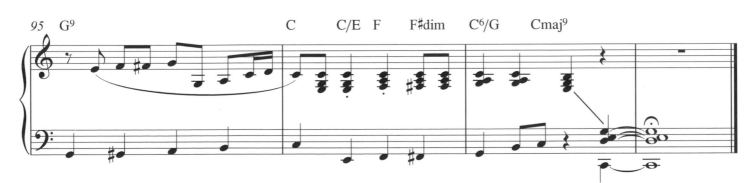

# Kinda Dukish

Music by Duke Ellington
Arranged by Carl Hudson

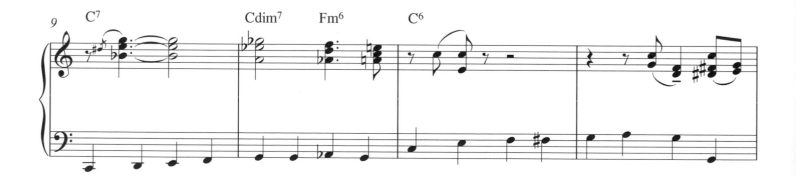

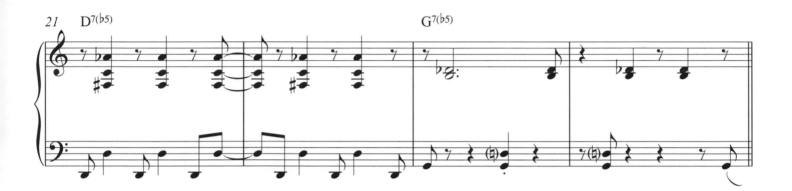

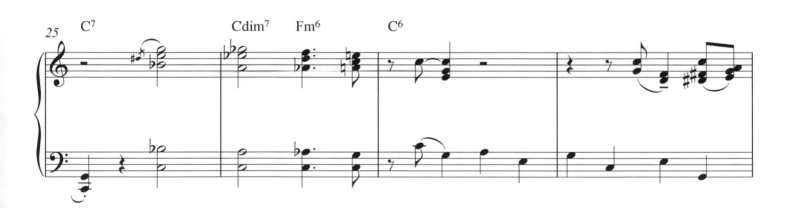

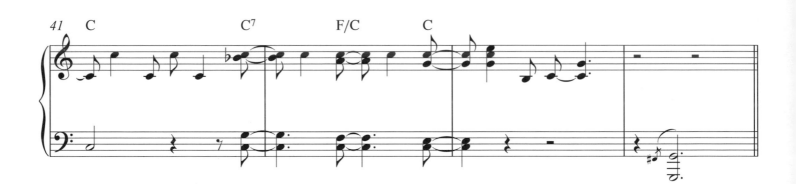

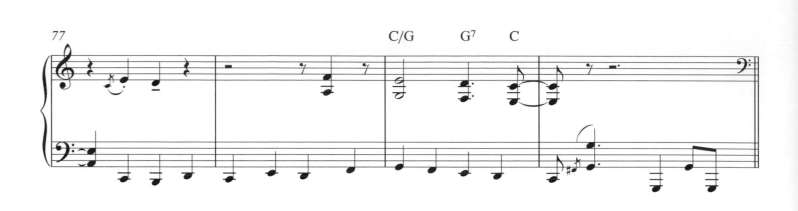

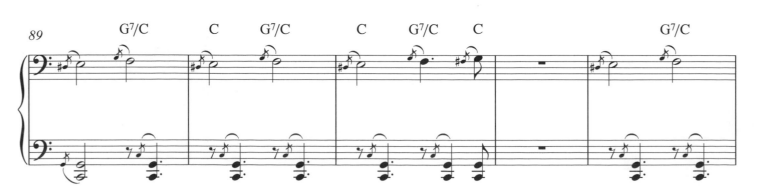

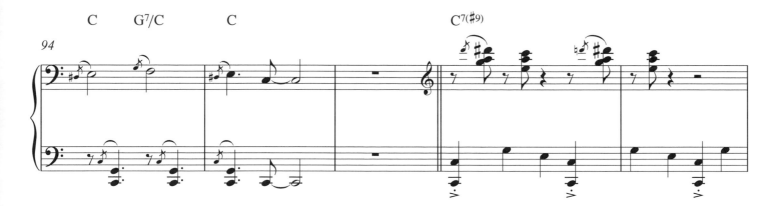

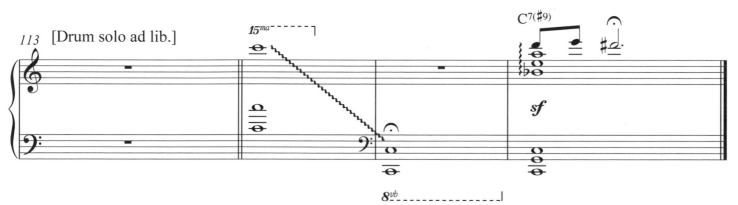

# Meditation

Music by Duke Ellington
Arranged by Carl Hudson

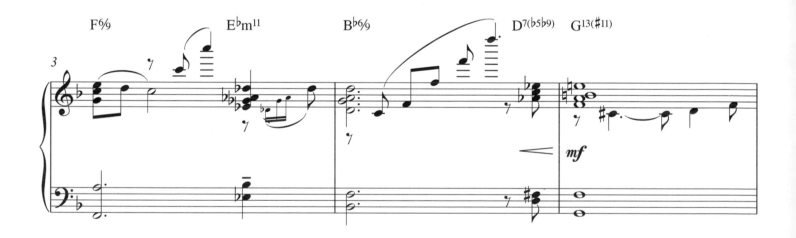

**più mosso**

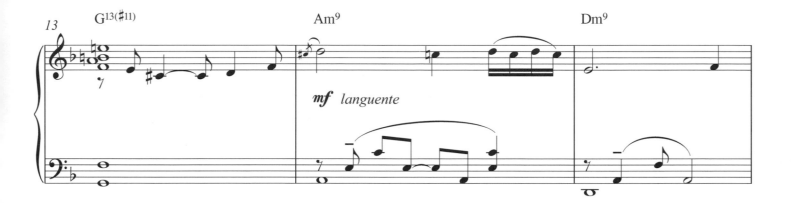

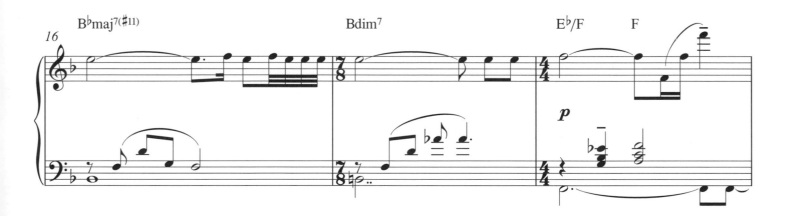

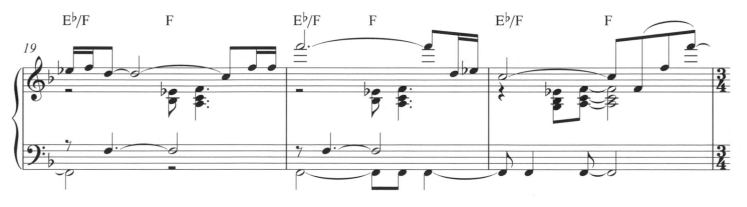

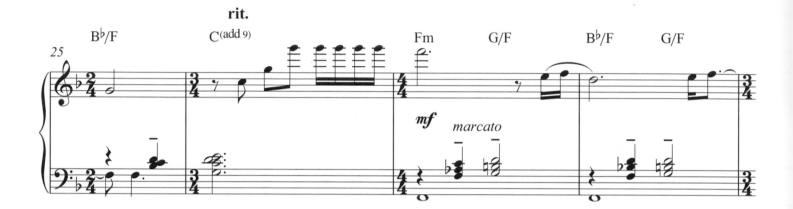

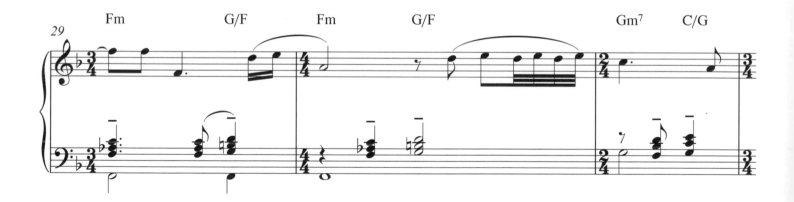

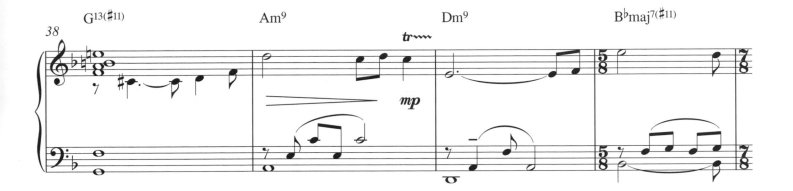

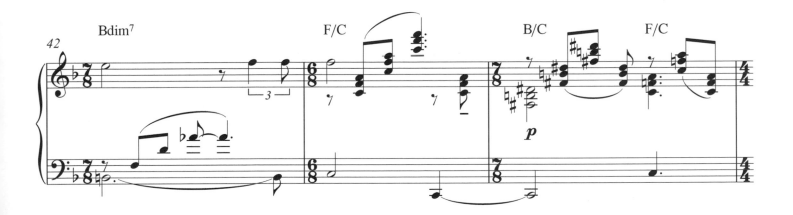

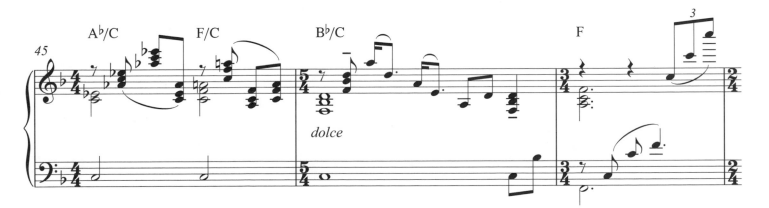

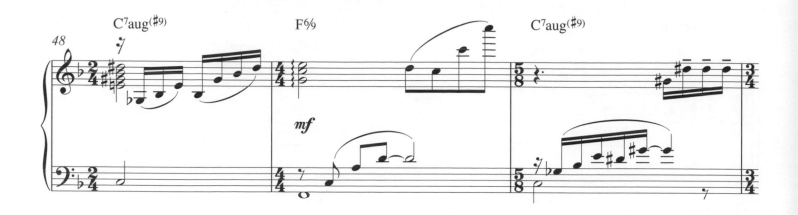

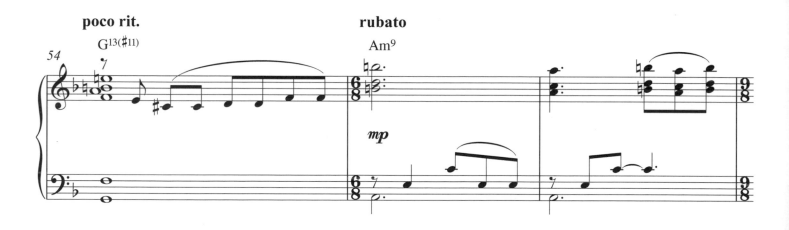

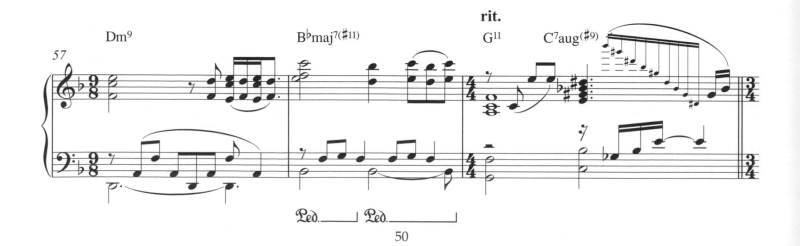

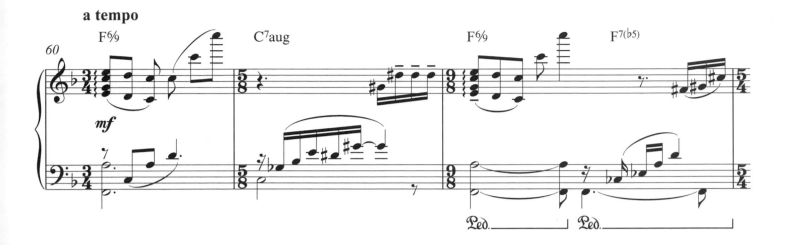

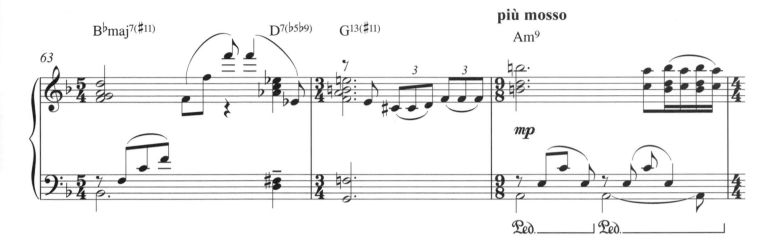

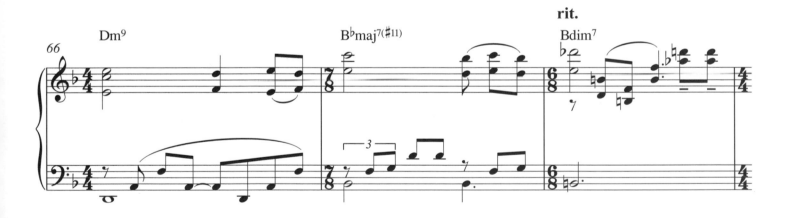

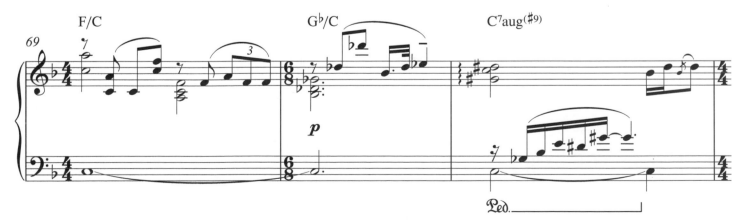

51

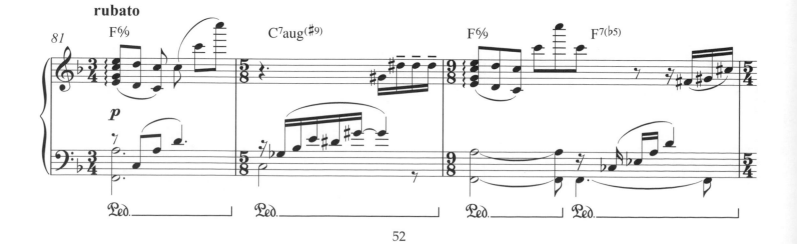

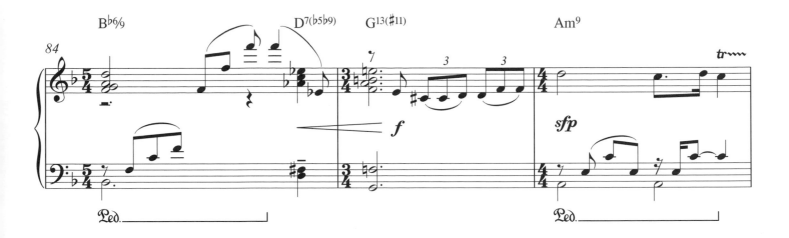

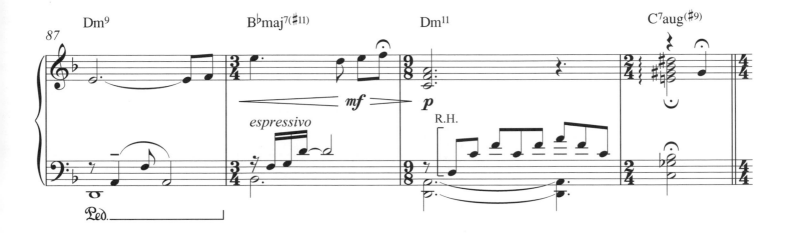

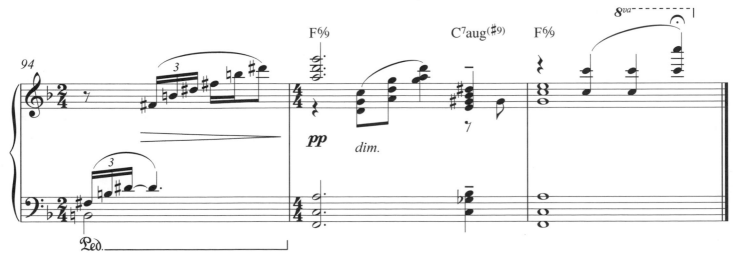

# New World A-Comin'

Music by Duke Ellington
Arranged by Carl Hudson

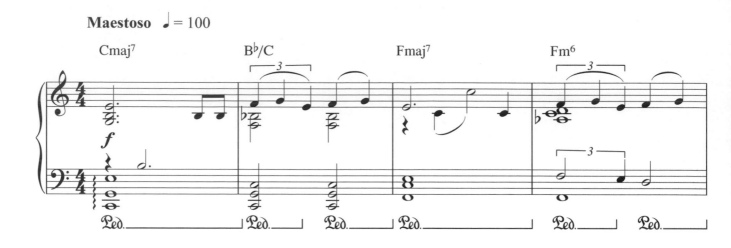

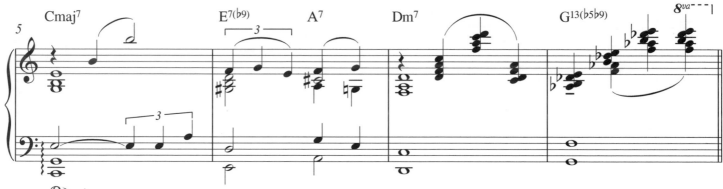

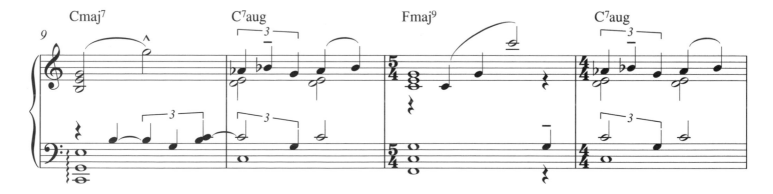

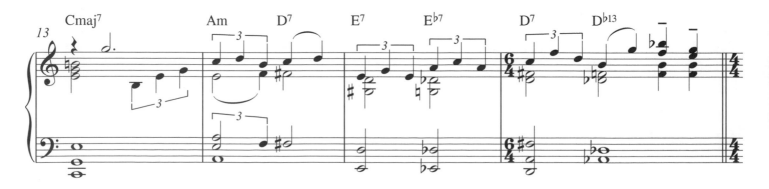

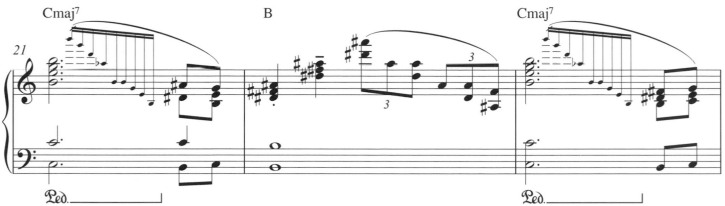

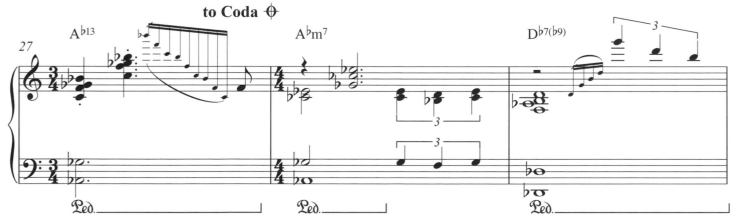

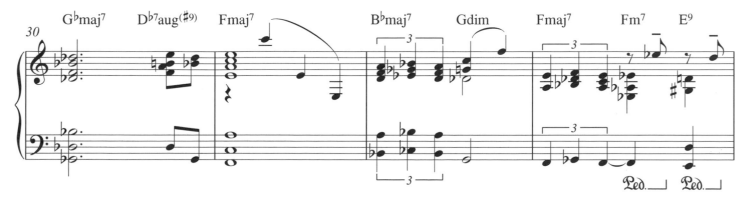

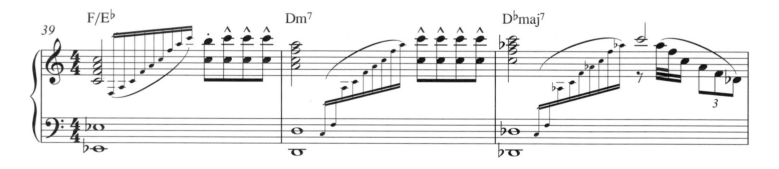

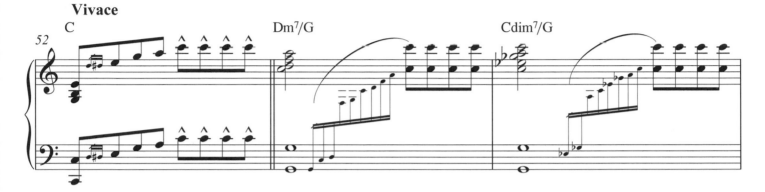

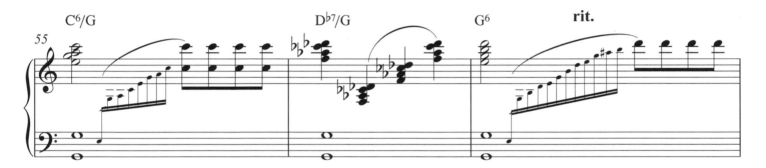

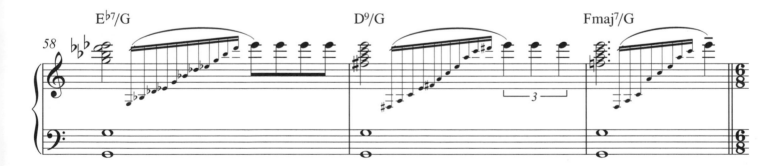

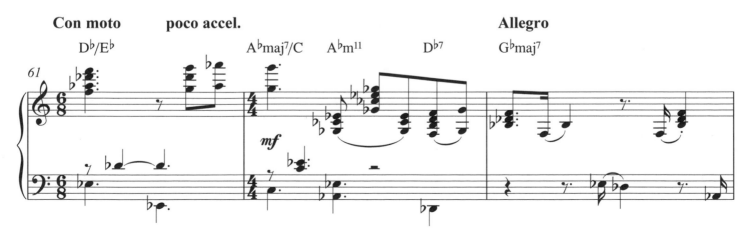

57

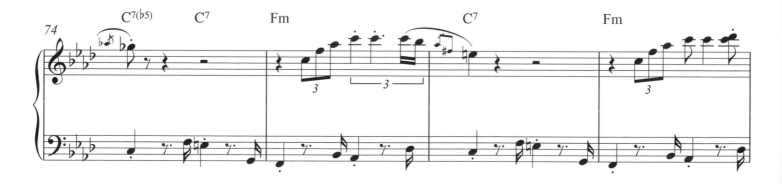

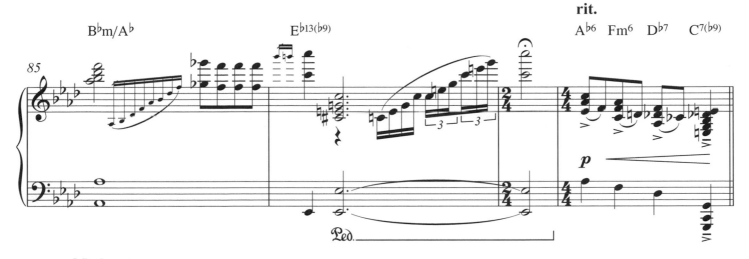

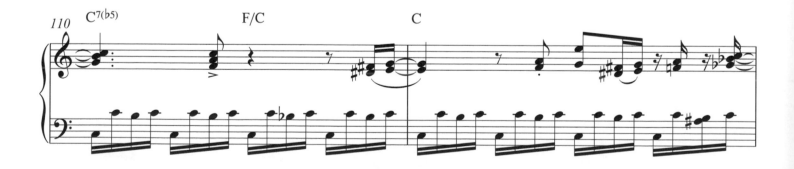

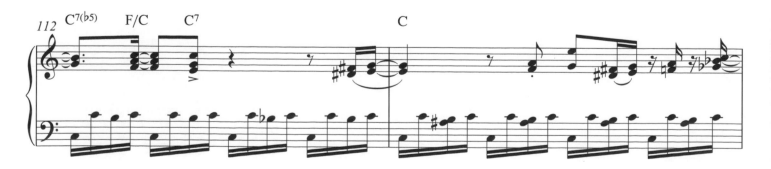

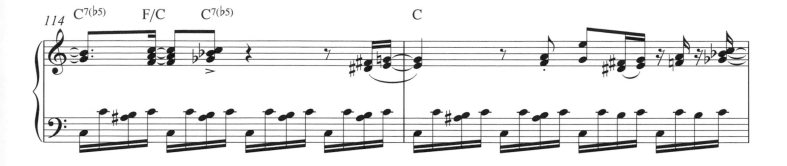

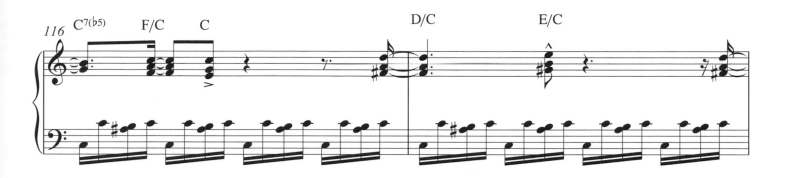

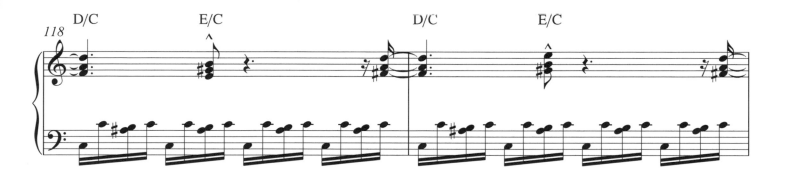

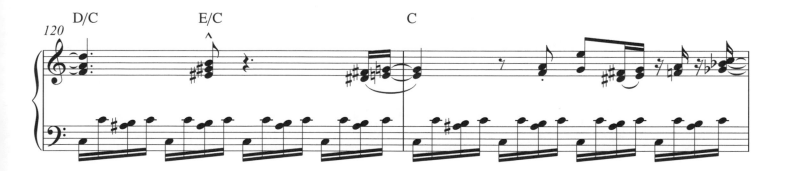

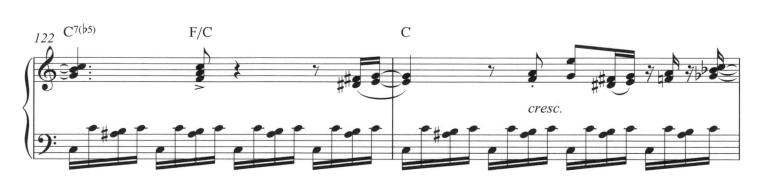

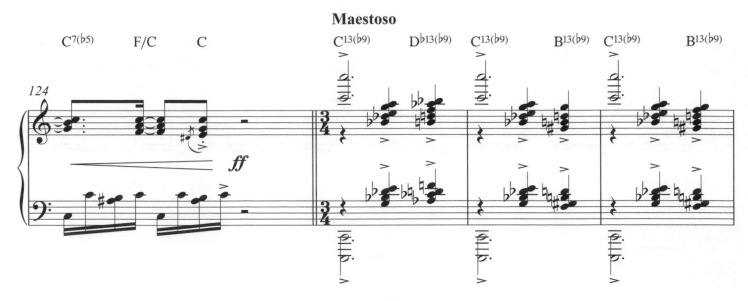

**Maestoso**

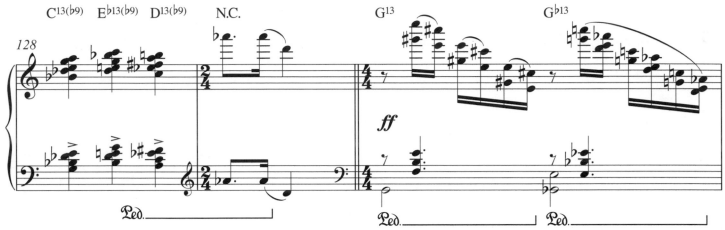

**Vivace**

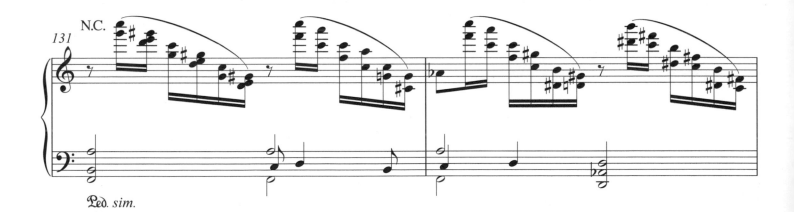

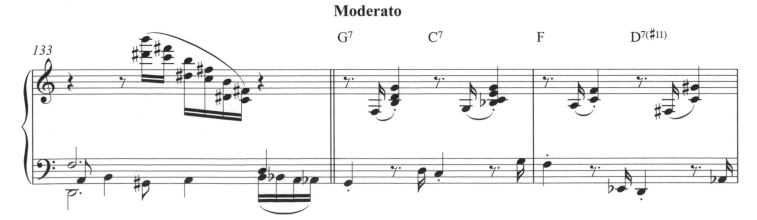

**Moderato**

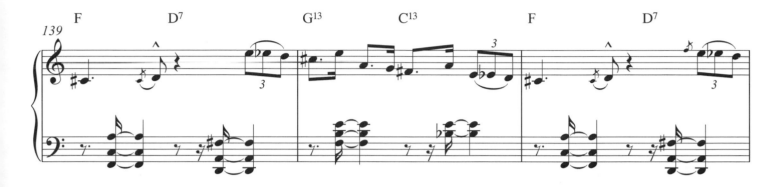

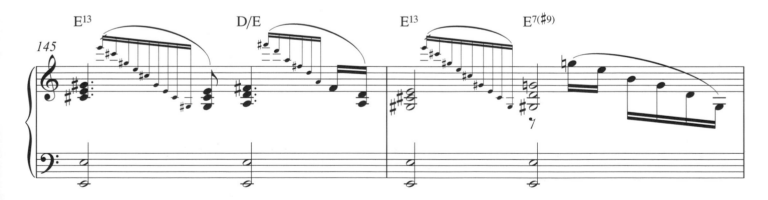

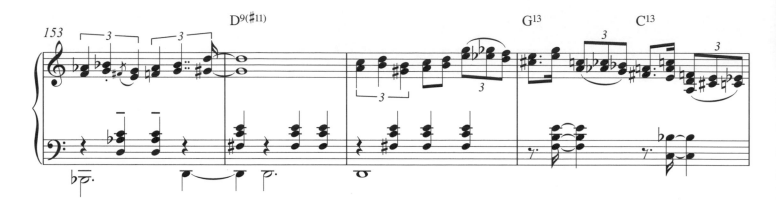

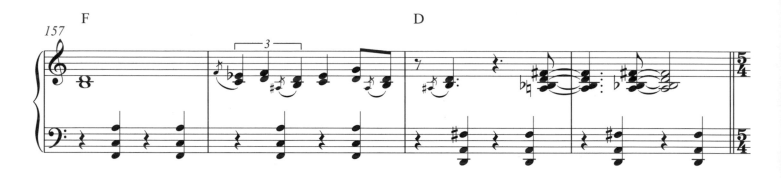

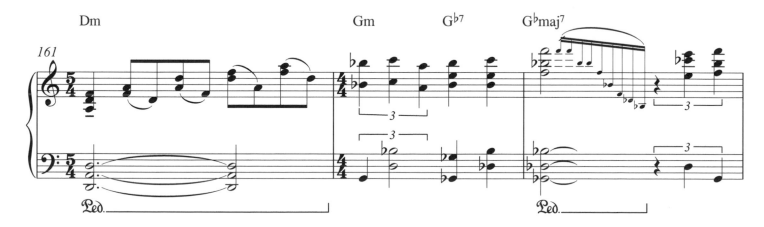

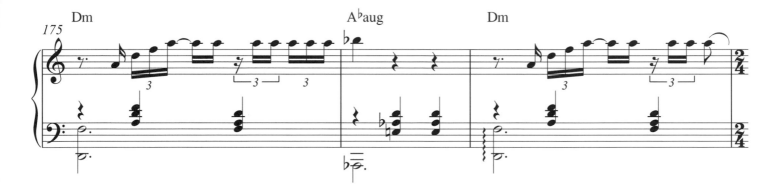

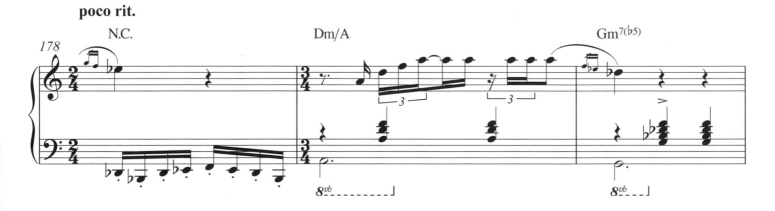

**Moderato**

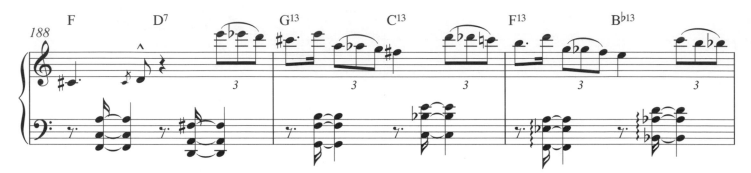

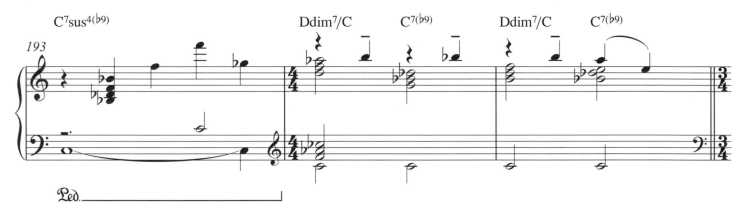

**Maestoso**

**D.S. al Coda**

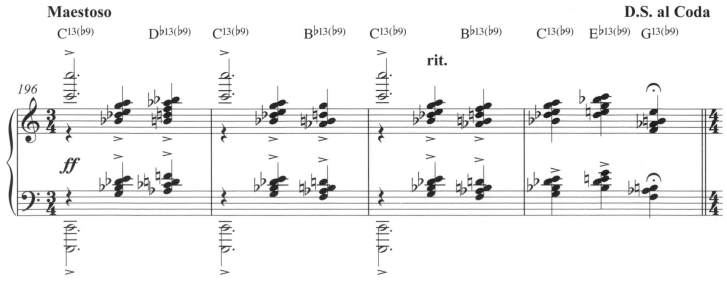

⊕ **Coda**

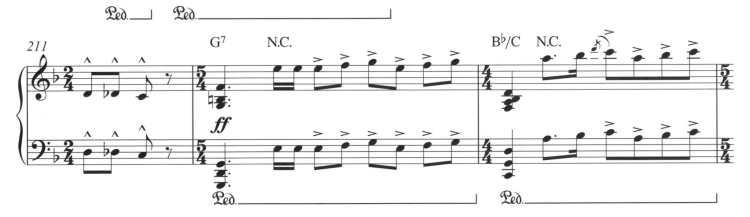

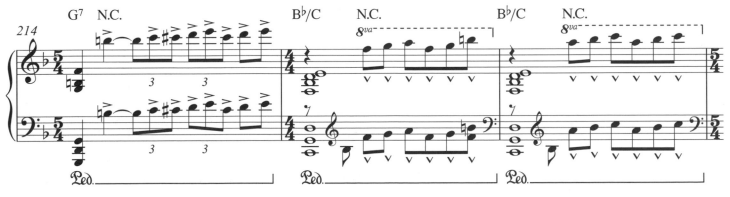

**Maestoso**

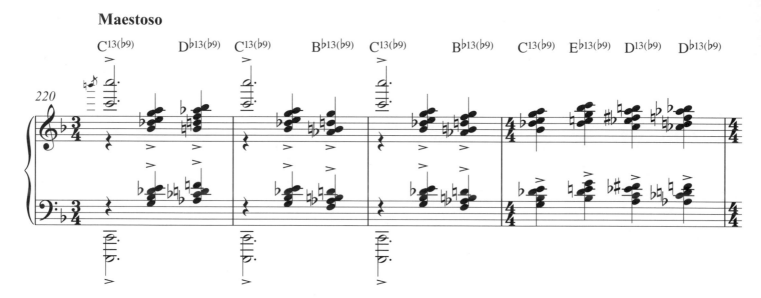

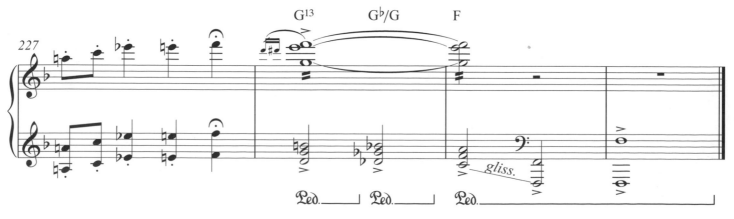

# Satin Doll
## (Instrumental Version)

Music by Duke Ellington

Arranged by Carl Hudson

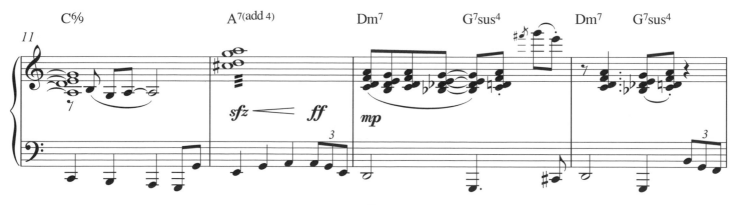

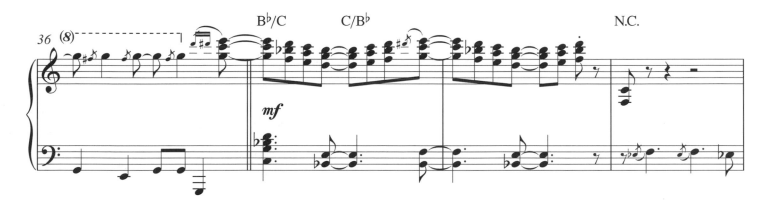

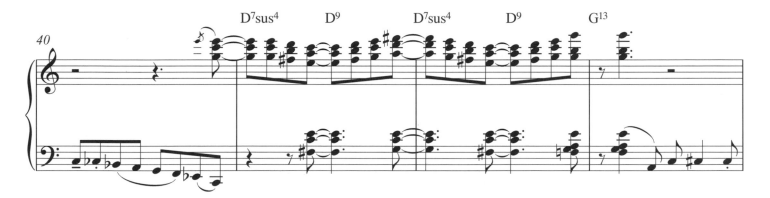

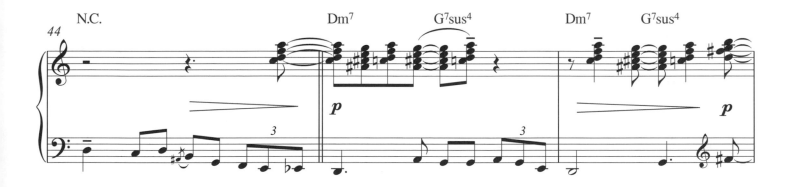

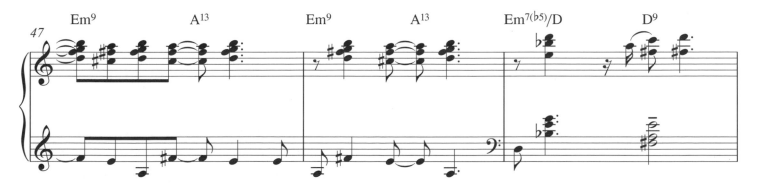

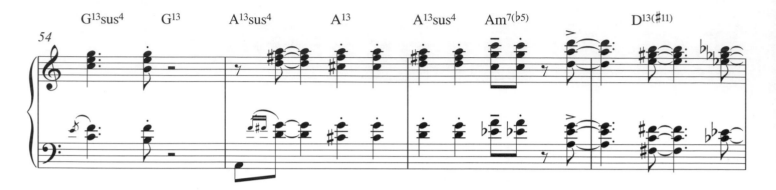

**D.S. al Coda**

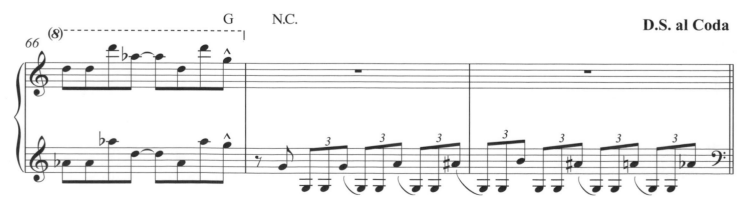

72

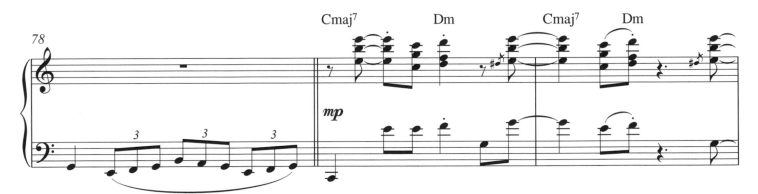
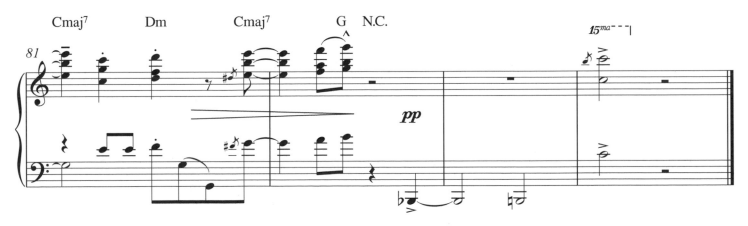

# Take The 'A' Train

Music by Billy Strayhorn
Arranged by Carl Hudson

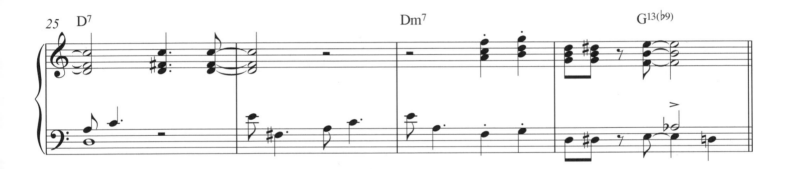

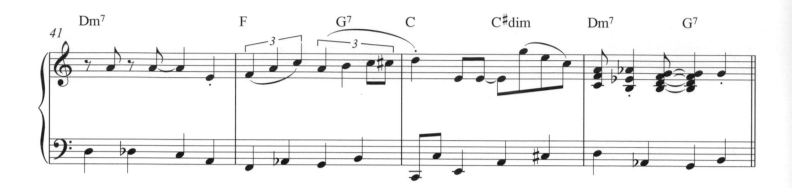

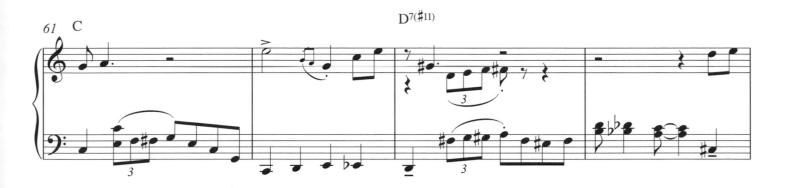

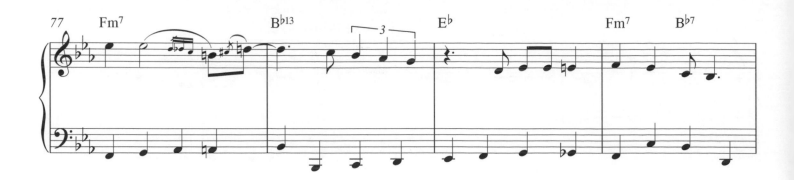

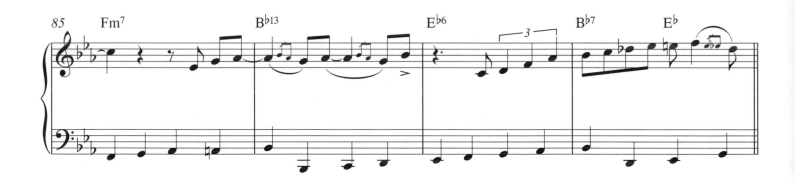

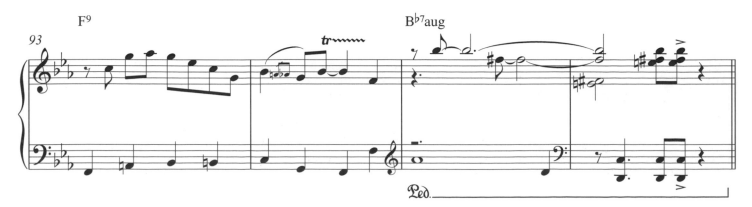

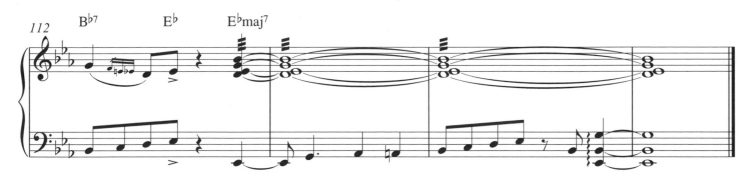

1 2 3 4 5 6 7 8 9

# CD TRACK LISTING

## 1. BLUES #1
(ELLINGTON)
EMI UNITED PARTNERSHIP LIMITED

## 2. 'C' JAM BLUES
(ELLINGTON)
EMI UNITED PARTNERSHIP LIMITED

## 3. COTTON TAIL
(ELLINGTON)
EMI UNITED PARTNERSHIP LIMITED

## 4. DON'T GET AROUND MUCH ANYMORE
(RUSSELL/ELLINGTON)
EMI ROBBINS CATALOG INC

## 5. KINDA DUKISH
(ELLINGTON)
EMI UNITED PARTNERSHIP LIMITED

## 6. MEDITATION
(ELLINGTON)
EMI UNITED PARTNERSHIP LIMITED

## 7. NEW WORLD A-COMIN'
(ELLINGTON)
EMI UNITED PARTNERSHIP LIMITED

## 8. SATIN DOLL (INSTRUMENTAL VERSION)
(ELLINGTON)
TEMPO MUSIC INC

## 9. TAKE THE 'A' TRAIN
(STRAYHORN)
STATE ONE MUSIC PUBLISHING UK

## 10. CARAVAN
(MILLS/ELLINGTON/TIZOL)
LAFLEUR MUSIC LIMITED